DEALING WITH CHILDHOOD TRAUMA AS AN ADULT

How to heal the long-term effects of your childhood pain that affects your mental health and happy life as an adult.

ROGGAN ALFRED

DEALING WITH CHILDHOOD TRAUMA AS AN ADULT

Copyright © 2022

By Roggan Alfred

All rights reserved.

DEDICATION

I dedicate this book to everyone suffering from the negative effects of childhood pains and violence.

It's for your sake and betterment that I wrote this book.

I LOVE YOU ALL.

DEALING WITH CHILDHOOD TRAUMA AS AN ADULT

LIST OF CONTENTS

WHAT IS TRAUMA IN CHILDHOOD?

   TOP TRAUMATIC CASES

CHILDREN'S TRAUMATIC STRESS SIGNS & SYMPTOMS

EFFECTS OF CHILD TRAUMA

   CHILDHOOD TRAUMA AND DISSOCIATION

   HOW DOES AN ATTACHMENT DISORDER AFFECT A CHILD?

HOW TO SUPPORT CHILDREN WHO HAVE BEEN TRAUMATIZED

OPTIONS FOR TREATMENT OF CHILDHOOD TRAUMA

ADULT SYMPTOMS OF PERSISTENT CHILDHOOD TRAUMA

   HOW TO DETERMINE IF CHILDHOOD TRAUMA STILL AFFECTS YOU TODAY (& HOW TO HEAL)

   TRAUMA'S LONG-TERM EFFECTS

   UNRESOLVED TRAUMA: WHAT IS IT?

SIGNS YOU MIGHT BE DEALING WITH CHILDHOOD TRAUMA'S LONG-TERM EFFECTS

RECOVERING FROM CHILDHOOD TRAUMA OF YOUR OWN

SUMMARY

BY ROGGAN ALFRED

INTRODUCTION

For any adult who had abuse or neglect as a child, '**Dealing with Childhood Trauma as an Adult'** is essential reading. It is a compendium of remedies that aid in spotting and illuminating undesirable patterns. The answers you discover might change your life, offering new insight, hope, and love.

Trauma is a very sensitive case that could affect a child's wellbeing till adult or even eternity. A child that was traumatized doesn't feel love as before, they might have problem with trust, being fearful for a little thing, wanting to be alone, overthinking, depression, etc. All these could result to negative life style or wrong decisions. On extreme cases, it could result to suicide.

If you have in anyway experienced severe pain in the past, living with a traumatized child, a parent or caregiver, this book is specially for you. This book will give you a clearer information what trauma is and lists of events that can be traumatizing to a child, it will guide you on how to cope with traumatized kids, and will also tell you what to do if you find out that your early childhood pains are still disturbing you as an adult. This is a special self-help book to overcome any emotional pain or other inflicting your life and enjoy the happiness of life in fullness.

Chapter 01

WHAT IS TRAUMA IN CHILDHOOD?

An incident that causes fear in children and is frequently violent, dangerous, or life-threatening is known as a childhood traumatic event.

Childhood trauma can manifest itself in many different ways depending on the circumstance and the person, but it is typically defined as any threatening or dangerous situation that a child experiences, witnesses, or learns about. However, not all trauma is created equal; what might be considered normal or readily addressed for one person may not be for another.

Throughout their lives, a lot of kids go through horrific experiences. By the age of 16, more than 67% of children will have gone through at least one traumatic event, according to the Substance Abuse and Mental Health Services

Administration (SAMHSA). When a child experiences trauma, it is crucial for parents or caregivers to seek support for the child in order to evaluate the impact and create a support plan.

There are numerous distinct circumstances that can result in trauma, which are also commonly referred to as adverse childhood experiences, or ACEs. Children may experience trauma from physical or sexual abuse, for instance. Children can suffer psychological effects from one-time occurrences like a vehicle accident, a natural disaster (like a storm), the death of a loved one, or a serious medical event.

Even though it might seem normal to an adult, ongoing stress such as living in a dangerous neighborhood or being the target of bullying can be traumatizing for a child. Childhood trauma might potentially arise from events that don't directly affect the youngster. For example, witnessing a loved one struggle with a serious medical condition can be very traumatic for children. This effect can also be caused by violent media.

An experience is not necessarily traumatic just because it is upsetting. For instance, a youngster will probably be impacted by a parent's divorce, but it won't necessarily be traumatic. It is simple to comprehend that some experiences are traumatizing, like enduring natural catastrophes, seeing domestic abuse, being sexually abused. However, two kids who experience the same thing, like a parent's death, may respond very differently. One child may eventually get over their sadness and learn to move on, while the other, probably the youngster may experience substantial behavioral changes or a warped perspective on the world as a result of uncontrollable emotions. Children who have experienced trauma may come to view the world through a fearful perspective. And long after the traumatic experience has passed, they could still feel fear, vulnerability, and insecurity.

DEALING WITH CHILDHOOD TRAUMA AS AN ADULT

Nobody has any way of knowing how each youngster will respond. Because of this, it is crucial for parents and other adults who are responsible for children to keep an eye on their actions and frequently inquire about what is going on in their lives. You must take the time to see things from their perspective, for this reason.

Although resilient, children are not formed of stone, and 46% of youngsters endure trauma at some point in their short lives. Adults frequently remark that children who experience trauma can be affected for the rest of their lives because they were so little when the event occurred.

That's not to imply that even if a youngster goes through a terrible ordeal, they won't be emotionally traumatized for life. However, it's crucial to know when a youngster may require professional assistance for coping with their trauma. Additionally, early intervention can stop the trauma's effects from lasting into adulthood.

The fact that there is no clear cause-and-effect relationship between childhood trauma and its effects is one of the first things to realize. There are many various kinds of trauma, and each person's response to the experience is based on a variety of variables, such as whether you were able to "process" the event with the appropriate support networks.

TOP TRAUMATIC CASES

Here are some of the more frequent events to give you a clearer picture of what trauma entails, which could be potentially distressing to a child:

- ✓ Sexual or physical abuse of children
- ✓ Observing domestic abuse
- ✓ Bullying
- ✓ Violence in communities or schools
- ✓ Natural catastrophes/Disasters
- ✓ Loss of a loved one as a result of different factors (e.g. death, divorce, separation)

- ✓ Neglect
- ✓ Severe ailment or incident
- ✓ Multiple traumas
- ✓ Trauma in early childhood
- ✓ Violence among intimate partners
- ✓ Medical injury
- ✓ Physical Neglect
- ✓ Refugee Trauma
- ✓ Trafficking in sex
- ✓ Theft and violence
- ✓ Grief after trauma
- ✓ Residing with a parent or caregiver who suffers from severe mental illness

This is not a comprehensive list; many experiences or incidents might be upsetting. It's crucial to remember that these are only typical examples of trauma; even if your experiences didn't resemble any of the things on this list, they were likely nonetheless upsetting to you.

How frequent is it?

Traumatic experiences affect millions of kids throughout the course of their lives. However, it's crucial for kids to understand that they're not alone when facing challenges. Many youngsters go through potentially traumatic situations in their homes, neighborhoods, and schools.

We refer to an experience a youngster has as a trauma when it leaves them feeling extremely threatened. Children and teenagers may experience a variety of traumatic incidents or trauma types.

Bullying

Bullying is a purposeful, unwanted action that is done with the objective to cause social, emotional, physical, and/or psychological harm to a victim who is frequently seen as being weaker.

Community Conflict

Community violence is being exposed to willful interpersonal violence performed in public by people who are not close to the victim.

Multiple Traumas

Complex trauma is the phrase used to describe both the wide-ranging, long-term impacts of exposing children to numerous traumatic events—often of an invasive, interpersonal type.

Disasters

In addition to extreme weather conditions like blizzards, droughts, excessive heat, and wind storms, natural catastrophes also include hurricanes, earthquakes, tornadoes, wildfires, tsunamis, and floods.

Trauma in early childhood

Early childhood trauma, in general, describes the painful events that happen to young children (0–6).

Violence among intimate partners

Domestic violence, also known as intimate partner violence (IPV), happens when someone intentionally causes injury to a former partner, a current partner, or a spouse.

Medical injury

Children and their families can experience a variety of psychological and physical reactions known as pediatric medical traumatic stress as a result of one or more medical occurrences.

Physical Neglect

Physical abuse happens when a parent or caregiver does something that causes a kid or teenager physical harm.

Refugee Trauma

Many refugees, especially children, have gone through war or persecution-related trauma that may continue to have an impact on their mental and physical health years after the events.

Sexual assault

Any interaction between a child and an adult (or another child) in which the child is exploited to sexually stimulate the perpetrator or an observer is considered child sexual abuse.

Trafficking in sex

The act of providing or getting anything of value (such as money, a place to live, food, clothing, drugs, etc.) in exchange for engaging in sexual activity with a person who is younger than 18 is known as child sex trafficking.

Theft and violence

By way of shootings, bombings, or other sorts of attacks, mass violence, acts of terrorism, or communal trauma can have a significant impact on families and children.

Grief after trauma

While many kids recover quickly from a death, other kids struggle with persistent issues that interfere with daily life and make it challenging to remember happy memories of their loved ones.

Chapter 02

CHILDREN'S TRAUMATIC STRESS SIGNS & SYMPTOMS

There are many different types of trauma and PTSD symptoms in youngsters. However, it is crucial for parents and other caregivers to keep a close check on kids to see if there are any changes in their behavior, academic performance, eating habits, or sleeping patterns, particularly after a life-changing event that can be upsetting to a kid.

Parents, caterers, or other people who interact with the child may spot one or more of the following potential trauma symptoms:

- ✓ Avoiding specific individuals, locations, and/or objects
- ✓ Modifications to academic performance
- ✓ Alterations in conduct
- ✓ Continuous anxiety or worry
- ✓ Trouble focusing
- ✓ Hyperactivity

- ✓ Increased melancholy or terrifying thoughts
- ✓ Isolation from friends and family and extreme independence\
- ✓ Overreacting to issues that were previously minor
- ✓ Staying away from activities they used to enjoy
- ✓ Focusing difficulties in previously simple situations
- ✓ Alterations in appetite
- ✓ Trouble sleeping
- ✓ Difficulties with authorities
- ✓ Volatile feelings (ex. sadness, anger, irritable)

Depending on the child's age, developmental stage, support network, and experiences, the response to traumatic events can vary. In many cases, the response may go beyond emotional symptoms. Traumatic experiences can have an impact on a child's brain development, which can have long-term effects on their physical, mental, and social development.

The impacts of childhood trauma can affect children or still affect you as an adult in a variety of ways, including:

Trauma-related stress disorder

Post-traumatic stress disorder (PTSD), which results from unresolved trauma, is a particularly unique mental health condition that does not always appear in those who encounter trauma, despite the fact that many people are aware of it. In actuality, after a stressful event, only 3% to 15% of girls and 1% to 6% of boys have PTSD.

It's crucial to emphasize that not all exposure to trauma results in a diagnosis of PTSD. Traumatic events in children can elicit a variety of reactions, and for some, they might induce Post-Traumatic Stress Disorder (PTSD). A person's likelihood of developing PTSD is significantly influenced by the length and perceived intensity of the trauma, as well as protective factors including the presence of safe and supportive environments.

However, anyone who has gone through tragedy can develop PTSD. These traumatic occurrences might be a single catastrophic event or a sequence of traumatic incidents, and both can have severe ramifications throughout adulthood.

Children who have PTSD may repeatedly replay the trauma in their brains. The trauma may also be reenacted in their play or they may shun anything that brings it up.

Having stated that, a few symptoms of PTSD include:

- ✓ Experiencing it again (flashbacks or nightmares)
- ✓ Avoidance
- ✓ Anxiety
- ✓ Depression
- ✓ Anger
- ✓ Difficulties with trust
- ✓ Dangerous or damaging behaviors
- ✓ Withdrawal

DEALING WITH CHILDHOOD TRAUMA AS AN ADULT

If any of these describe you as an adult without any apparent explanation, there may be cause for concern as you may be suffering with unresolved childhood PTSD.

Relations and attachment

Problems building ties and relationships are another red flag of childhood trauma that persists into adulthood. For instance, if a loved one or caregiver was responsible for the trauma you experienced as a youngster, you might grow to distrust people. This mistrust may persist into adulthood and have an impact on your capacity to build relationships with other people.

Or perhaps you routinely associate with negative individuals because that is what you know from your upbringing (a victim of child abuse may marry an abusive spouse, for example).

A dependable loved one, a caretaker, or even a family member is often involved in childhood tragedies. Trust, safety, and security can all suffer from these incidents. People could find it very difficult to keep up with long-standing relationships or start up fresh, wholesome ones.

Challenges at School

Traumatic experience exposure affects learning for the rest of one's life and may have a detrimental effect on a child's short- and long-term academic success. Different ways that the detrimental influence can be seen are possible. Inattentiveness, disrespect for teachers and other authority figures, avoidance of school and schoolwork, and a general deterioration in academic performance are all possible among children.

In any event, if you find it difficult to build strong bonds with your classmates, this could be an indication of unresolved childhood trauma.

Emotional control and reactions

The inability to control your emotions may be another repercussion of childhood trauma. This issue may present itself in a variety of ways, including:

- ✓ Unrestrained rage
- ✓ Anxiety
- ✓ Depression
- ✓ A difficulty communicating your emotions

Mental health

The risk of many mental health issues is increased by trauma, particularly childhood trauma. In addition to a higher likelihood of developing post-traumatic stress disorder, the events may also lead to other mental health issues like:

- ✓ Control of anger issues
- ✓ Emotional angst
- ✓ High stress levels
- ✓ Psychotic illnesses
- ✓ Disorders caused by drug misuse
- ✓ Anxiety conditions
- ✓ Depressive illness

Physical wellbeing

While childhood trauma can have a negative impact on your mental and emotional well-being, it can also have a negative impact on your physical health.

Trauma effects can also emerge physically as children age and enter adulthood. Traumatic events can have long-lasting detrimental impacts on health, happiness, and opportunities, according to the Center for Disease Control (CDC). Adverse childhood experiences can raise the risk of physical health issues like cancer, heart disease, diabetes, and suicide.

The chance of developing a chronic illness later in life increases with the number of traumatic events a kid has, according to a 2015 study reported in the American Journal of Preventive Medicine. It specifically mentions how recurring trauma raises a child's likelihood of developing. For instance, studies suggest that children who experienced abuse were more likely to experience major health problems, such as:

- ✓ Diabetes
- ✓ Cardiovascular disease
- ✓ Asthma
- ✓ Stroke
- ✓ Cancer

A stressful event that a youngster goes through can hinder their physical growth. Their immunological and central nervous systems' growth may be hampered by the stress, making it more difficult for them to reach their full potential.

Children might think they missed signs that the painful incident was coming. They become too alert in searching for clues that something unpleasant is about to happen again in an effort to avert further traumas.

Various Effects

The effects of trauma on children, both direct and indirect, are almost limitless. For instance, a traumatized person may struggle in school and ultimately leave out early, which results in a low income, substandard housing, and exposure to further stress. Trauma affects more than just the person who experiences it. Many times, the events and their effects cause their family, friends, coworkers, and classmates to struggle.

Complex traumatized children may even become disassociated. Dissociation entails mentally separating oneself from the experience. They might imagine that they are outside of their bodies and watching it from somewhere else or they may lose memory of the experience, resulting in memory gaps.

Research published in Psychiatric Times further notes that the prevalence of suicide attempts is significantly higher in adults who experienced traumas such as physical abuse, sexual abuse, and parental domestic violence as a child.

Adults who endured childhood trauma have been demonstrated to make significantly more suicide attempts.

I strongly advise you to seek for help so that specialists can help you break the hold that childhood trauma still has on your life if any of these descriptions apply to you.

EFFECTS OF CHILD TRAUMA
CHILDHOOD TRAUMA AND DISSOCIATION

Relationship Impacts

A child's relationship with their caregivers—whether they be parents, grandparents, or other familial or non-familial adults—is crucial to their mental and physical health. The bond children have with their caregivers can help them learn to trust others, manage emotions, and positively engage with the world around them.

However, if a youngster goes through a trauma that teaches them they can't rely on or trust that caregiver, they're likely to think the world is terrifying and people are dangerous. The ability to develop relationships throughout their youth and into adulthood becomes extremely challenging as a result of this instruction.

Traumatized children are more prone to struggle in love relationships as adults.

According to a 2017 study published in the Journal of Family Psychology, even when still in the honeymoon stage, marriages with partners who have a history of abusing children tend to be less fulfilling.

Childhood trauma can affect children for the rest of their lives in many different ways, including emotionally, physically, and in their relationships, if it is not treated.

HOW DOES AN ATTACHMENT DISORDER AFFECT A CHILD?

Various Effects

The effects of childhood trauma might occasionally go beyond relationships and physical or mental health. For instance, several studies have found a link between unfavorable childhood experiences and a higher likelihood of becoming a criminal offender by the age of 35, frequently committing significant and violent crimes.

Additional effects could be:

- ✓ Being more readily "set off" and reacting more strongly
- ✓ Taking part in risky activities (such as driving at high speeds or unsafe sex)
- ✓ Not being able to anticipate or prepare for the future
- ✓ Greater likelihood of self-harm
- ✓ Impulse control issues
- ✓ A low sense of self
- ✓ Difficulty with logic or problem-solving
- ✓ Holistic child development as it relates to well-being
- ✓ Changes in child brain development

Children who experience traumatic incidents may also be less prepared to raise their own children in the future.

Childhood trauma not addressed

Untreated childhood trauma might result in long-lasting problems since its effects are frequently not healed. A person's ability to avoid some of the harmful effects of trauma, even biologically, is also limited if they do not receive treatment.

Study discovered that people with untreated childhood trauma had higher levels of glucocorticoid resistance. Depression and glucocorticoid resistance are closely related. These results imply that trauma neglect may, both directly and indirectly, contribute to the emergence of depression.

Chapter 03

HOW TO SUPPORT CHILDREN WHO HAVE BEEN TRAUMATIZED

As a parent or caregiver, it can be difficult to watch your child cope with a traumatic situation. Parents and other caregivers must make sure that children who have been through traumatic events receive the assistance they require in order to thrive despite the trauma.

A child's chance of developing suicidal thoughts can be decreased by providing them with social support, which can help lessen the effects of trauma on them.

Following a distressing occurrence, here are some strategies for assisting your child's trauma recovery:

- ✓ Encourage the child to express and be accepted for their feelings.

- ✓ Help them realize they are not to blame.
- ✓ Respond to their inquiries honestly.
- ✓ Assure the youngster that you will take all necessary precautions to keep them safe.
- ✓ As much as you can, maintain a daily schedule.
- ✓ Please be understanding as each child heals at their own rate.
- ✓ As a parent or caretaker, familiarize yourself with the subject of trauma.
- ✓ Learn what triggers your child.
- ✓ Visit a certified mental health therapist with your child to determine the needs of the youngster.
- ✓ If your child is given medication, make sure they take it consistently and according to the directions.
- ✓ When dealing with potentially traumatic situations, provide children with a place where they feel emotionally safe to express themselves.
- ✓ As a parent or caregiver, practice taking care of yourself. If necessary, seek out mental health support.
- ✓ Work with your child's school to ensure that your child receives the proper academic support when dealing with social and emotional challenges.

- ✓ Abuse and trauma can have long-lasting effects. Recovery can be aided by therapy. Therapy and medication can help if your child is having trouble healing from trauma.

The child may be referred for therapies like cognitive behavioral therapy, play therapy, or family counseling, depending on their age and requirements. Medication may also be a possibility in some circumstances, such as when PTSD has been diagnosed, to assist treat the symptoms.

As a parent or caregiver, it is crucial to offer support to your child if they have gone through a traumatic event and to also get them expert help to determine their requirements. To determine the symptoms and confirm that what your child is going through is not a physical or medical ailment, the first step should be to take him or her to the pediatrician.

DEALING WITH CHILDHOOD TRAUMA AS AN ADULT

After addressing the physical reasons of the symptoms, you should look for mental health therapies to assist your child. Numerous pediatricians can give patients the phone numbers of counselors that focus on working with kids and teenagers. Take your time and find a mental health professional with experience in trauma-informed care who specializes in treating children and adolescents while searching for someone to treat childhood trauma. Getting a list of providers from your insurance provider, getting a referral from your child's pediatrician, and/or getting a recommendation from a coworker, friend, or family member are all ways you can find mental health providers who specialize in treating children and adolescents.

When looking for a mental health specialist to help your child after a traumatic occurrence, keep the following factors in mind:

- ✓ Verify the therapist's acceptance of new patients.
- ✓ Make sure the service places a strong emphasis on children's mental health.

- ✓ Make sure they employ trauma-informed approaches, particularly when working with kids and teenagers.
- ✓ To support your child in the academic environment, encourage cooperation with the child's therapist and school.

OPTIONS FOR TREATMENT OF CHILDHOOD TRAUMA

It is crucial for parents or other caregivers to seek out mental health assistance when a child has a traumatic event in order to determine the child's requirements. Depending on the mental health diagnosis, the course of treatment for children who have experienced trauma may change. Depending on the diagnosis also, therapy such as cognitive behavioral approaches, in particular trauma-focused cognitive behavior therapy, as well as techniques developmentally suitable for children and adolescents are frequently used to treat childhood trauma.

Children who are exposed to stressful situations may also develop additional disorders, such as anxiety, sadness, or even ADHD, in addition to PTSD. If parents or other adults suspect their kid is exhibiting any of these symptoms, they should speak with their child's pediatrician or a child psychiatrist. Finding a mental health practitioner with experience working with children who have experienced trauma is essential when parents or caregivers are looking for treatment for their children.

Treatment Options

The following evidence-based therapies can be used to address childhood trauma:

The Child and Family Traumatic Stress Intervention (CFTSI) aims to lessen post-traumatic stress symptoms while supporting parents and caregivers by improving communication and giving kids healthy coping mechanisms to use in spite of any reactions they may experience as a result of the traumatic event.

The fundamental objective of cognitive processing therapy (CPT) is to assist the client in reducing ideas that are restrictive and obstacles to living despite the traumatic event(s).

In order to lessen the overall influence that the trauma has on the child's life, narrative exposure therapy (NET) aims to reframe traumatic events so that they can be contextualized. This therapeutic approach involves having kids narrate life experiences while focusing on their good attributes.

Trauma-Focused Cognitive Behavioral Therapy (TF-CBT) teaches children and their parents/caregivers how to express themselves, learn cognitive coping mechanisms to deal with stressors, develop relaxation skills, create and process trauma narratives, and manage behaviors that may be harmful to outcomes. It is specifically created for children.

Sensorimotor Psychotherapy: By incorporating movement into conventional talk therapy, sensorimotor psychotherapy seeks to address and repair persistent psychological and physical challenges brought on by trauma.

Medication

Selective serotonin reuptake inhibitors are a class of medications that are frequently used to treat PTSD in the beginning (SSRIs). SSRIs are acknowledged as effective treatments for treating both mood and anxiety disorders. Depending on the child's symptoms, other drug classes may also be taken into consideration.

SSRIs are not safe for everyone, particularly when co-occurring diseases necessitate drugs that could have negative drug interactions. Any time children are given medications, they should have an age-appropriate discussion about them with them.

Personal Changes

It's crucial to remember that children also need expert assistance when considering lifestyle modifications to support youngsters who have undergone traumatic situations. Avoiding re-traumatizing children is a key objective when deciding on lifestyle modifications.

For kids, adopting the following lifestyle modifications could be a terrific addition to a treatment program created by a mental health specialist:

- ✓ Make sure the youngster sleeps an appropriate amount for his/her age.
- ✓ Teach the youngster relaxation skills that are appropriate for his or her stage of development (e.g. deep breathing techniques, positive visualization, positive affirmations).
- ✓ Encourage kids to exercise and participate in enjoyable activities.
- ✓ Practice consuming nutritious foods that will recharge you.
- ✓ Assist them in reframing unfavorable ideas.
- ✓ Encourage them to recognize the individuals that make up their support network and to make time for them.

Chapter 04

ADULT SYMPTOMS OF PERSISTENT CHILDHOOD TRAUMA

HOW TO DETERMINE IF CHILDHOOD TRAUMA STILL AFFECTS YOU TODAY (& HOW TO HEAL)

If you have PTSD from childhood abuse, it may be challenging to address the root causes of the trauma in order to ease adult symptoms.

How can maltreatment inflicted on children lead to post-traumatic stress disorder in adults?

• Do you find it difficult to deal with the trauma from your early years?

• Do you find it difficult to recover from childhood trauma?

• Do you still struggle with making decisions?

DEALING WITH CHILDHOOD TRAUMA AS AN ADULT

• Do you abuse any medications to numb your pain? Do you consume too much food or liquids?

These are only a few of the problems maltreated children deal with as adults.

You might not even be aware that you were harassed. It's possible for you to think that your parents didn't mean it, that they weren't wise enough to know better, or that other people had it far worse. It's likely that you are unaware of the connection between your present problems and the past.

Some people will be able to process and recover from their childhood trauma with the passage of time, maturity, or professional treatment. Other people will continue to be affected by the unfavorable childhood experiences and carry these emotions into adulthood.

DEALING WITH CHILDHOOD TRAUMA AS AN ADULT

Sometimes the past doesn't stay in its proper place. It may surprise you if you went through childhood trauma that the issues you dealt with as a youngster are still bothering you today. You might be concerned that your traumatic childhood would affect your happiness, relationships, or perhaps other aspects of your professional life. Perhaps you are unsure about how to begin learning how to heal.

Recently, you haven't felt like yourself. And you've been wondering: Do you have unresolved trauma from your youth? You assumed it had ended. However, is your childhood trauma be affecting your adult life and giving you the impression that everything is upside down? If so, why now, then?

But recently, your anxiety has returned. Occasionally on the verge of panic, feelings of depression are starting to dominate. You might even feel like hiding out in a shell.

How might your trauma still be unattended to? What's the deal here?

TRAUMA'S LONG-TERM EFFECTS

A person's physical, emotional, social, and cognitive capacities may be affected by trauma at any point in their lives. Untreated trauma frequently has a number of long-term repercussions, including:

- ✓ Alcoholism
- ✓ Neurological and biological conditions
- ✓ Chronic illnesses of anxiety or depression
- ✓ Smoking cigarettes
- ✓ Leaving school early
- ✓ Wrong usage of drugs
- ✓ A quick death
- ✓ High-risk actions (e.g. HIV exposure, sexually transmitted diseases)
- ✓ Obesity
- ✓ Suicide

UNRESOLVED TRAUMA: WHAT IS IT?

Perhaps you've heard the term "unresolved trauma," but what does it actually mean? You have told yourself that it is all behind you and that you have moved on. Is that not enough?

Perhaps you've also received therapy. How could you possibly still be in pain?

When you were traumatized as a child, it may remain with you forever. You might even say it becomes ingrained in your bones. Even if you push the memories aside and aren't aware of them, they nevertheless have an impact on your physical symptoms, your love life, and your low self-esteem. Many traumatized kids feel that they've always been on their own and try to solve their own problems as best they can. The issue is that you can only accomplish so much on your own. The most severe impacts of childhood trauma frequently remain "unresolved" because of this. Even if you have undergone counseling, you could still wonder why you keep remembering the trauma.

DEALING WITH CHILDHOOD TRAUMA AS AN ADULT

Awfully, many therapists lack expertise in treating childhood trauma, which is what you require to get to the heart of your formative experiences. Sure, no specific formula exists for dealing with unresolved childhood trauma. You've had your own experiences, and they've each had a unique impact on you.

Unfortunately, the causes of your childhood trauma continue to be unaddressed. Those signs can disappear for a period. However, stress that upsets your emotions or an incident that comes too near to reminding you of your past trauma can bring you back to the initial experiences.

The reasons why "the past" isn't always the past.

Even though your trauma is technically "in the past," you can't truly move past traumatic events that happened to you as a child unless you fully comprehend how they continue to influence your present-day relationships, experiences, and symptoms. Even when we attempt not to, we tend to have a "compulsion to repeat." Because of this, you can find yourself in relationships that make you think of ones that once caused you trauma.

Your symptoms or habits could manifest in a variety of ways. Once more, these are very specific to you. The past is never simply the past, and that is what matters. Your childhood trauma may continue to be "unresolved" until you have received assistance figuring out precisely how the roots of your past are still present in the present.

What leads to trauma in young children?

Trauma can sometimes be quite visible, such as in cases of physical or sexual assault. However, there are other forms of childhood trauma that you might not even recognize as trauma.

One or more of the following may have affected you: parental neglect/uncaring parents, parent loss, a life-threatening childhood sickness, learning handicap that made you question your abilities, excessive sibling load, emotionally distant or uncaring parents, or even your parent's own childhood trauma are all traumatic experiences. Neglect is very painful – neglect from childhood refers to not having your emotional or physical needs met. This can be a result of your parents' stress and distraction.

Or because one or both of them have a mental disorder, which makes them want you to act as the "parent," look after the other children, or perform a lot more household duties than any youngster should.

Whatever the reason, your desires for nurturing and care were ignored, disregarded, or met with a tremendous deal of resentment. Never should a parent take advantage of their child for their own purposes. The physical and emotional requirements of a child should come first. If yours didn't, you were ignored.

Early in life, losing a parent to death or abandonment is traumatic. No matter how well-cared-for you were by other family members or your parent who is still alive, this type of loss is profound. That loss lives on much more strongly within you if it wasn't acknowledged, heard, or permitted. You required a moment to grieve, and perhaps you still do. Because you too early discovered that a required loved one could vanish or be taken away. You develop a fear of losing.

This is a vulnerable moment, even if your parent passed away while you were in your early 20s. Because proximity and need imply the possibility of loss, you can fear becoming close. The majority of unresolved childhood trauma impairs one's self-worth and causes anxiety.

Did you have a major sickness as a child? If so, you were probably hospitalized or isolated at home.

DEALING WITH CHILDHOOD TRAUMA AS AN ADULT

You were cut off from customary social interactions, which undoubtedly made you feel lonely and perhaps even self-conscious about your differences. Because of it, you could now feel less socially secure and unsure of where you fit in. Separation from parents, frequently traumatic medical procedures, and dread are among side effects of hospitalization. You might experience ongoing anxiety as a result.

It helps if you had strong emotional ties to your parents and they were readily available and encouraging. Otherwise, you can now experience insecurity in significant connections.

If you had learning difficulties, such as dyslexia, ADHD, or any other learning disorder, you probably felt different or negatively compared yourself to the other children. If learning issues went untreated and you didn't receive enough support, it can be very challenging to live with them. Even incredibly smart children eventually come to believe that they are not at all smart.

Your self-image is greatly impacted by this. You might have put a lot of effort into getting better and better while battling obstacles outside of your control. Or perhaps you gave up and caved.

Either you still have a problem with imperfection or you always try to please others while never feeling satisfied. Or you feel stuck in a cycle of perpetual relapse. Even if you believe your learning issues have been resolved, they can still affect you.

Are you one of many children in your family? Did you feel as though there was never enough for everyone? That frequently occurs in households with many kids. Particularly if you were all born near to one another, resources are scarce. In particular, if your mother was overworked, under pressure, and distracted with the always demanding siblings. Or, if you were the oldest, you would be expected to look after the younger children.

Being the youngest among many siblings can also be stressful, despite how loving you might have thought your family was (or perhaps you didn't feel that way at all).

You might have felt disoriented in the crowd. Not heard or observed, pushed aside, excluded, and utterly by myself. A youngster could feel emotionally abandoned and unwanted as a result of this sibling relationship. You might even believe that in order to be appreciated, you must put aside your needs or be the giver. You might also sense a profound longing for the love you think you can't and won't find.

When a mother is distant or unavailable, the impacts of having too many siblings are even more noticeable. A parent who is unreachable is distressing. Children require attention, validation, being held, and emotional support. When you wait, watch, and long to be heard, the impacts can endure a lifetime.

DEALING WITH CHILDHOOD TRAUMA AS AN ADULT

Perhaps you are scared of your wants and unsure of whether you will be loved. Perhaps you also learned to keep your distance and to not have high expectations. Maybe your parent was worried, one who was untrusting, anticipated disaster, hid from people, or was fearful.

Without you even realizing it, your parent's anxiety may have seeped into your pores, leaving you frightened, preoccupied, and suffering from the same anxieties.

A parent who was emotionally aloof or nervous was likely traumatized as well.

Transgenerational trauma is unquestionably a thing.

It is handed down from parent to child, from unconscious mind to unconscious mind, if your mom or dad had a terrible upbringing that was also unresolved.

DEALING WITH CHILDHOOD TRAUMA AS AN ADULT

Children are at risk. You grabbed it. You too were impacted.

Parents who experienced trauma continue to experience trauma. They frequently can't give you their whole attention or start to identify with the abuser who also victimized them.

Or, if your parent(s) survived a terrible incident, like the Holocaust, the dread and unfathomable losses may continue to haunt them and you.

If these multiple traumatizing events go unresolved, their consequences continue to harm you and can last well into adulthood in a variety of different ways.

What impact does it have on you as an adult?

Even though you've made every effort to move on, there is still a traumatized child living inside of you, and this might cause childhood trauma to occasionally seep into your adult life. This kid part of you still carries your trauma and suffering if you haven't had the correct kind of therapy or enough support to deal with your trauma.

Perhaps you're not constantly aware of it, but when you're under stress, childhood trauma symptoms might manifest. Or if something in your life serves as a subliminal or overt reminder of something that happened to you when you were a youngster.

Your symptoms are a result of childhood trauma. Depression, ear strikes, an eating dysfunction, relationship apprehensions, catastrophe fears, and obsessional worries. You might have trouble trusting people, low self-esteem, judgmental fears, a relentless need to please others, angry outbursts, or persistent social anxiety symptoms.

Can childhood trauma be healed?

Yes, unresolved childhood trauma can be healed. Seek out therapy with someone psychoanalytically or psychodynamically trained.

A therapist who understands the impact of childhood experiences on adult life, particularly traumatic ones. Have several consultations to see if you feel empathically understood. If not, continue looking for a safe therapeutic place, one in which you may create trust, is vital. Your therapist must understand and allow for your skepticism at first.

All sentiments need to be permitted, supported, and heard. These emotions could include dread, panic, intense sadness, and rage.

Your therapy must progress at your rate of choice. You shouldn't be forced, criticized, or expected to go more quickly than you are capable of.

DEALING WITH CHILDHOOD TRAUMA AS AN ADULT

What you need is a delicate, compassionate, and empathic reaction. You need to feel protected and seen by the small traumatized child who still resides inside of you. Empathy, however, is not everything. Additionally, you require a person with expertise in how childhood trauma affects an individual's life. Someone who is very aware of your effects.

You don't have to put up with the symptoms' tendency to flare up in response to stress or bad memories. You will recover from unresolved childhood trauma when you receive this type of therapy and can give yourself the time you require.

Chapter 05

SIGNS YOU MIGHT BE DEALING WITH CHILDHOOD TRAUMA'S LONG-TERM EFFECTS

Children can return to a healthy state of functioning even though there may be some degree of suffering following a traumatic experience, and some children are less influenced by their surroundings than others.

It is never too late to obtain help if childhood trauma has had detrimental repercussions. Trauma treatment can still be helpful and effective, whether you adopted a teenager who was abused more than ten years ago or you never sought treatment for the traumatic events you went through forty years ago.

For information about support groups and treatment centers in your region, call the Substance Abuse and Mental Health Services Administration (SAMHSA) National Helpline at

DEALING WITH CHILDHOOD TRAUMA AS AN ADULT

1-800-662-4357 if you or a loved one is suffering from childhood trauma.

If you have PTSD from childhood abuse, it may be challenging to address the root causes of the trauma in order to ease adult symptoms. However, the following questions can be addressed:

- How can maltreatment inflicted on children lead to post-traumatic stress disorder in adults?
- Do you find it difficult to deal with the trauma from your early years?
- Do you find it difficult to recover from childhood trauma?
- Do you still struggle with making decisions?
- Do you abuse any medications to numb your pain? Do you consume too much food or liquids?

These are only a few of the problems maltreated children deal with as adults. You might not even be aware that you were harassed. It's possible for you to think that your parents didn't mean it, that they weren't wise enough to know better, or that other people had it far worse. It's likely that you are unaware of the connection between your present problems and the past.

It's shocking how common childhood trauma is in the United States; by the time they turn 16, more than two-thirds of kids had experienced at least one traumatic event. Trauma, which includes everything from bullying to assault, is a regrettable part of growing up for many kids, and its effects can linger well into adulthood.

RECOVERING FROM CHILDHOOD TRAUMA OF YOUR OWN

Since post-traumatic stress disorder (PTSD) may impair practically every part of your life, living with it might feel a lot like being imprisoned. There are ways to free yourself, and we go over those here.

You struggle with depression and have tried numerous drugs in vain to get well. I urge you not to give up because there are still solutions available even if this is known as treatment-resistant depression.

There are provisions of a variety of mental health services to aid in coming to terms with a troubled background. To enable you to move past painful memories and pursue a happy and healthy life, it is our mission to assist you in making peace with them.

In order to begin started, it's critical to notice the warning indications that a former childhood trauma might still be following you around. With that in mind, let's go through some of the prevalent red flags here.

Obsessive-compulsive disorder (OCD) is a complex anxiety disease that affects 1% to 2% of people in the United States, yet there is a lot of misconceptions out there about it. What you need to know is as follows.

Major depressive disorder is characterized by overwhelming sadness, a sense of helplessness, and a loss of interest in activities you formerly enjoyed. However, the mental health condition can also cause other, less well-known symptoms.

There are various steps you may take to help you deal better if you had trauma as a child and still need to go through the healing process. They include:

- ✓ Spending time with the helpful individuals in your life.

- ✓ Maintaining a regular eating and sleeping routine.
- ✓ Engaging in physical activities.
- ✓ Avoiding drugs and booze.

You can begin to heal by speaking with a mental health expert. Numerous trauma-informed therapies, such as acceptance and commitment therapy (ACT), eye movement desensitization and reprocessing (EMDR), and cognitive processing therapy (CPT), among others, may be employed as therapeutic choices.

You could also wish to get in touch with trustworthy groups that can assist people who have survived childhood trauma. One choice is the Substance Abuse and Mental Health Services Administration's (SAMHSA) Disaster Distress Helpline. Another option if you'd rather text someone is the Crisis Text Line.

SUMMARY

In conclusion, childhood/child trauma can be very devastating. Sometimes, the feeling and agony might follow a child to adulthood, and might even last forever. Whereas some easily forget or let go of their traumatic experience(s). In all, do your possible best not to be a source of your child's or other child's trauma, help your child or other children to overcome traumatic experiences and feel joy (in a situation of loss) and wanted again (in a situation of neglect). In a case of disaster, comfort them and convince them that the world in not really a place of war. Show your kids and other children around you care, treat them with love and concern (let them feel the love and care around them, let them feel wanted and appreciated). The emotional trauma children pass through are much more than any hunger.

In a situation that you were traumatized in the past for one reason or the other, comfort yourself. Relying on the pains of the past might hinder you of the joy of today and the

DEALING WITH CHILDHOOD TRAUMA AS AN ADULT

happiness of tomorrow. Of course, forgetting the past has never been easy, but constantly remind yourself that you really need to let go of any experiences that will negatively have an impact on your soul, mind and body.

It will be unworthy to cause other children to face same pain you faced in the past, just because you felt everyone should have a share in your pain. On the other hand, it will be worst to think that the world is full of evil people because of the negative experience you had with someone in the past. Erase the scars from your mind, and you will find yourself in a midst of angels in human form. Indeed, the world is full of good and pleasant people. Seek medical help when the need arises. Be around those that makes you happy and feel loved. Find someone or a group where you can freely share your fear and find consolation. You shouldn't die of depression and agony of the past. You deserve a happy life – your child deserves a happy life – every kid deserves a happy life.

Printed in Great Britain
by Amazon